COASTERS
2000
by
Bernard McCall

INTRODUCTION

Since beginning to write *Coastal Shipping* magazine in 1994, I have received a steady supply of photographs from readers but it is not possible to include all of them in the magazine. In order to give the photographs the wide audience which they deserve, and to supplement the dearth of pictorial shipping books, I thought that it would be a good idea to produce and publish the present volume.

The original concept was simple. I would select two photographs from each week of the year with the bonus of a colour section for those photographs taken during the sunny summer weeks of mid-year. The concept may have been simple - its execution has not been so simple. Problem number 1 - what summer? what sun? Problem number 2(a) - some weeks resulted in a wealth of excellent material - which to choose? Problem number 2(b) - some weeks produced almost no material! To make matters worse, I also wished to illustrate as wide a variety of locations as possible, and use the work of as many different photographers as possible.

In the event, the concept has proved much more difficult to bring to fruition than I had imagined. I hope that readers will enjoy the book and accept that it is as close as possible to the original ideal. If readers do like the idea and the resulting book, it could become an annual publication.

Acknowledgments

Firstly, I must offer my sincere and grateful thanks to those who have made their photographs available and thus enabled the book to reflect coastal shipping in this first year of the new millennium. I also acknowledge the help of *Lloyd's Register of Shipping* and *Marine News* (Journal of the World Ship Society) in tracing the details of ships featured. Notable among those always ready to answer specific queries have been Richard Potter, Dag Bakka Jr and Bent Mikkelsen. As always I want to thank Gil Mayes for reading preliminary drafts of the book, for his constant encouragement and constructive criticism and for checking facts. Any errors which remain are my own responsibility. I also wish to thank my family for their patience, and the staff of Dalton Printers for their splendid contribution to the final appearance of the book.

Bernard McCall, Portishead   March 2001

Published by Bernard McCall, 400 Nore Road, Portishead, Bristol, BS20 8EZ, England.
Telephone/fax : 01275 846178. e-mail : bmccall@globalnet.co.uk
All distribution enquiries should be addressed to the publisher.

Printed by Dalton Printers, Dalton House, Thesiger Street, Cathays, Cardiff, CF24 4BN
Telephone : 02920 236832; fax : 02920 666516

ISBN : 1-902953-03-7

*Front cover : Brunel's famous suspension bridge in Bristol forms the backdrop to the Russian **Leonid Leonov** as she approaches the Cumberland Basin on 25 February.* *(Bernard McCall)*

There can be no better way to begin this look at coastal shipping during the year 2000 than a New Year's Day view. The location is Sharpness and the weather was eerily mysterious. A misty start to the day turned into a sunny morning. The only ship to move on the day's early afternoon tide was the **Gudrun II** (ATG, 1599gt/77), inward bound from St Malo with a cargo of 1750 tonnes of fertiliser in bulk. As she came up the River Severn, a cloud bank hovered above her and she was in shadow as she made her approach to the entrance lock. At the same time, the opposite bank of the river was suddenly obliterated by mist. *(Dominic McCall)*

There was, no doubt, a distinct chill in the air when the **Shala** (RUS, 2829gt/86) was photographed at the Russian port of Kaliningrad on 2 January. There is a hint of ice but the dock is clearly almost ice-free on this winter day. It is only in the last decade, following the collapse of the communist government, that the port has been open to non-Russian vessels. It was the base for a large section of the Soviet navy, hence the need to keep ships of other nations well clear. The **Shala** is a sea/river vessel of the "Volgo-Don" class and was built at Oltenitze in Romania. This class was originally intended for river and canal work but some of the ships were shortened in the mid-1990s to make them more suitable for sea passages. This ship was built as the **Volgo-Don 5094** and was renamed in 1994 when she was shortened.
(Barry Standerline)

After completion of loading a cargo of limestone, the hatch covers of the **Nandia** (CYP, 1939gt/82) are being closed as she makes ready to depart from Llysfaen Jetty at Llanddulas on 6 January. She is a representative of the Type 110 class built at the J. J. Sietas yard on the outskirts of Hamburg between 1981 and 1986 and under the name **Katja** was handed over to her initial owners on 11 December 1982. In 199o, she was renamed **Birte Wehr** and then became **Humber Star** in 1995. At this time she was registered at Funafuti and flew the Tuvalu flag. In January 1999, she reverted to the name **Birte Wehr** but six months later was sold and was renamed **Nandia** by her Cypriot flag operators.
(John P Evans)

The year began and ended with far better weather, at least in north-west Europe, than that experienced during the so-called summer months. Conditions for photography were certainly ideal as the **Duisburg** (ATG, 1943gt/86) passed Tilbury Landing Stage on her way up the River Thames on 8 January. Built at the Damen shipyard in Bergum as **Wilma**, she was renamed **Erika H** in 1992, **Phini** in 1997 and took her present name at the end of June 1999.   *(Kevin Bassett)*

The port of Sutton Bridge lies on the River Nene in eastern England. Following its re-activation in 1987, it has taken some of the trade from Wisbech a few kilometres further upriver. The wharf at Sutton Bridge can accommodate four coasters and all berths were occupied on 10 January. Vessels seen are, from left to right, the **Simone** (DEU, 1710gt/82), **Veritas** (NLD, 1666gt/93), **Ilona G** (999gt/90) and **Sea Clyde** (ATG, 1683gt/84). The **Simone** was built by Detlef Hegemann Rolandwerft, Bremen; the **Veritas** is a product of the Peters' Scheepsbouw yard at Kampen a/d Ijssel; and **Sea Clyde** was built as **Petena** by the Cassens yard at Emden. Her change of name came when she was taken on charter by Seacon in 1998.   *(John P Robinson)*

The ***Iberian Ocean*** (BHS, 1029gt/79) was built by J W Cook & Co, Wivenhoe, as ***Birkenhead Miller*** and in 1982 she joined the fleet of Crescent Shipping, at that time better known under its alternative title of London & Rochester Trading Co Ltd, by whom she was renamed ***Zealence***. After five years in this fleet, she was taken over by Cardiff-based Charles M Willie & Co (Shipping) Ltd who gave her the name ***Iberian Ocean*** to reflect her usual trading area. She is often found trading from Spain and Portugal to the UK with timber and timber products and returning with clay loaded at ports in Devon or Cornwall. She was photographed on 15 January as she left Teignmouth. The pilot cutter is in close attendance as she passes the gently sloping beach at Shaldon, a popular location for ship photographers. *(Dominic McCall)*

Following the departure of the ***Iberian Ocean***, the ***Freya*** (PMD, 1548gt/91) arrived in ballast from Newport. She has kept her original name since construction at the Heusden yard of Vervako BV although it is only recently that she has transferred from the German flag to the increasingly popular "convenience" flag of Madeira. The was her first visit to Teignmouth and she loaded a cargo of ball clay for delivery to the French port of Le Légue. *(Dominic McCall)*

Coastal tankers from the fleet of Crescent Shipping make regular calls to ports on the east coast of Ireland usually with oil products from Milford Haven. The **Breaksea** (992gt/85) was photographed on 22 January as she prepared to leave Dundalk. She had arrived the previous day with a cargo of gas oil from Milford Haven. She was built at the Nordsøværftet yard in Ringkøbing on the west coast of Denmark and has kept her original name. *(Jim Brodigan)*

The almost perfect reflection in the water of the River Neath suggests that 27 January was a still day. The **Ewald** (DEU, 1599gt/99) is at Giants Wharf, Briton Ferry, loading anthracite for delivery to Neuss on the River Rhine. She was a new ship, built by BV Scheepswerf De Kaap, Meppel, a shipyard which builds mainly inland waterway vessels. *(Bill Moore)*

The three day period between 2 and 4 February was one of unusual coaster activity along the Manchester Ship Canal. The reason was that three coasters operated by James Fisher which had been laid up in Birkenhead were taken in tow along the Canal to prepare them for re-entry into service. On 2 February, the **Solway Fisher** (IRL, 1707gt/77) moved up the Canal in tow of the tug **Vanguard**. The **Solway Fisher** was built at the Gruno Shipyard, in Foxhol, for Dutch owners and was lengthened in 1980. Four years later, she was sold to Arklow Shipping and was renamed **Arklow Valley**, transferring to the Irish flag. She remained under the Irish flag when demise chartered to Capt Frank Allen's nascent Dundalk Shipowners in 1991. She was renamed **Rockpoint** and her port of registry was changed to Dundalk. The Dundalk owners faced financial problems in the mid-1990s and the ship was transferred to James Fisher & Sons (Liverpool) Ltd. She retained her Irish registry after being renamed **Solway Fisher**. In this photograph, she is passing Cadishead on the outskirts of Manchester. *(John Slavin)*

On 3 February, it was the turn of the **Briarthorn** (1576gt/80), ex **Craigallian**-89, to make her way up to Manchester and she was photographed as she passed Runcorn. This ship was built by Richards at Lowestoft. *(Neil Burns)*

Passing Tilbury Ness as she departs from the Thames on 10 February is the **Pia Theresa** (DIS, 563gt/76). She is bound for Århus and had arrived earlier in the day from Harlingen. She provides us with a first look at a ship which has been converted for she began life as a conventional cargo ship named **Arroi**, one of a large class of basically similar standard ships built at the now-closed Nordsøværftet shipyard in Ringkøbing. In 1982, she was renamed **Limfjord** and then was sold in 1984 and was converted to a tanker, mainly for the carriage of vegetable oils in six tanks. She is operated by Herning Shipping A/S and has had the name **Pia Theresa** since 1985.

(Kevin Bassett)

Ships are occasionally called upon to carry large deck cargoes and forward visibility can be a problem. After calling at Copenhagen for bunkers, the **Skantic** (VCT, 1081gt/74) is seen leaving the port on 11 February with a large pipe reel and what seems to be a barge as deck cargo. Navigational visibility has been improved by the addition of a temporary wheelhouse built on the forward section of the barge. The ship was built as the **Skanlith** by Frederikshavn Værft og Tordok A/S and was sold and renamed **Skanlill** in 1983, taking her present name in February 1999. She was understood to be on a voyage from Paldiski to Bergen when she made her call at Copenhagen.

(the late Ove Nielsen)

The **Nariman** (SYR, 1665gt/72) was built at the Gebr van Diepen yard in Waterhuizen, Holland, for German owners and was named **Jasenitz** until 1996 when he was sold to A. M. Ismail Shipping Agency Ltd, based in the Syrian port of Tartous. With two holds and two hatches served by a crane amidships and two derricks, she is an ideal general cargo carrier. One assumes that her owners will trade her mainly in the Mediterranean so her ice-strengthened hull will have little advantage there. She is seen arriving at Casablanca on 15 February.

(Barry Standerline)

As noted on page 4, the **Sea Clyde** (ATG, 1843gt/84) was built at the Cassens shipyard in Emden as **Petena** and was renamed in 1998 when chartered by Seacon Ltd. An ideal vessel for use in the steel trades, she is strengthened for the carriage of heavy cargoes and is also strengthened for navigation in ice. She also has a useful container carrying capacity of 102 TEUs. She is seen in Tilbury Dock on 13 February, having arrived from Europoort three days earlier. Her Seacon charter ended in the autumn.

(Gavin Rayfield, courtesy Port of London, Tilbury)

The **Alteland** (DEU, 2996gt/95) was launched under the name **Patria** by the J. J. Sietas yard. On a sunny 21 February, she was photographed in the River Elbe when outward bound from Hamburg to the Swedish port of Gefle. At the time of the photograph this ship was on charter to Team Lines for its feeder service from Hamburg and Bremerhaven to Sweden and Finland. There was occasional confusion in the Baltic because a larger vessel of the same name was working on a similar route - indeed the vessels had crossed in the Kiel Canal only six days previously. Most of the ships in the Team Lines fleet are owned by one of the four German shipping companies which formed the fleet in 1991. However, the **Alteland** is owned by Hermann and Gerda Koppelmann.

(Krispen Atkinson)

The fact that this book contains several photographs of Russian ships or ships controlled by Russian interests illustrates the strong influence exerted by this country in the seaborne trade of Europe, both north and south. Since the collapse of the USSR a decade ago, several classes of ships previously seen only on the vast Russian inland waterways system have emerged and become familiar in much more widespread trading patterns. One such class is the "ST" class, characterised by the bridge-forward design. An example of the class is the **Ruza-3**, (RUS, 1627gt/86), ex **ST-1314**-86, which was built at Volodarskiy Shipyard, Rybinsk. She is seen here in the very unusual location of Convoys Wharf at Deptford on the south bank of the River Thames, a wharf normally visited only by roll-on/roll-off ships delivering paper and forest products. She had arrived from an unknown location on the River Rhine. Convoys Wharf closed to all shipping later in the year, its trade being transferred to docks at Tilbury and Chatham.

(Peter Hutchison)

The highlight of the year for the compiler of this book, and for many enthusiasts in the south-west of England was the arrival of the *Leonid Leonov* (RUS, 2264gt/95) in Bristol's City Docks on 25 February. She arrived to load equipment from a local brewery which had closed, the tanks and associated equipment being taken to St Petersburg. Tug assistance on the passages both up and down the River Avon was provided by the appropriately-named ***Avongarth***. In this view, the *Leonid Leonov* is negotiating the tricky section of Horseshoe Bend as she made her way down the Avon from Bristol on 28 February. *(John Southwood)*

The sun shone, at least in the Bristol Channel area, throughout the weekend that the *Leonid Leonov* was in port. On 26 February, Beck's ***Vedette*** (NLD, 2033gt/90) arrived at Sharpness in glorious sunshine to load a cargo of 3197 tonnes of wheat for Warrenpoint. She was built at the Bodewes yard in Hoogezand, from where many Dutch coasters have emanated over the years.

(Dominic McCall)

The Cornish port of Par has always been associated with the export of china clay and has been operated by English China Clay Ltd. That familiar title has disappeared following the company's takeover by French owners and has been replaced by the name Imerys. These new owners made it known that it was difficult to justify the continued existence of both Par and Fowey as china clay exporting ports and that closure of Par would be likely unless new cargoes could be obtained. Thankfully, the port has indeed been able to attract new cargoes, one of these being the import of timber. Discharging a cargo from Riga on 5 March was the **Antares** (NIS, 1373gt/69), built by Husumer Schiffswerft as **Bele**. Renamed **Tor Ireland** in 1973, she reverted to her original name briefly in 1975 before becoming **Amazone** and in 1986 she was renamed **Gardwill**. She took her present identity in 1991. *(Courtesy Port of Par)*

The **Vyacheslav Denisov** (RUS, 1798gt/71) was one of a class of 20 ships built for the former USSR government-controlled merchant fleet in order to carry timber from the vast forest areas to other parts of northern Europe. Known as the "Soviet Warrior" class after the lead ship, **Sovietskiy Voin**, many of the ships were transferred out of Russian-flag operation during the 1990s and the ship featured here joined several of her sisters under the Cambodian flag, though it is assumed that there is still a strong Russian influence in the actual ownership. The change came in 1997 when she was renamed **Silva**. Two Russian shipyards were used to build the ships; the **Silva** was built at the Okean Shipyard in Nikolayev and she was the last in the series to be built. This fine photograph shows her heading south through the Fair Isle Gap on 6 March with what appears to be a full cargo of timber. She had spent the previous two days in Lerwick but little cargo, if any, seems to have been discharged there so her call may have been for other reasons. She had loaded in Riga and was heading for Belfast. *(Richard Jones)*

The ***Rosita Maria*** (NIS, 2316gt/77), an example of the J. J. Sietas Type 81 standard class, has been a popular vessel in the short-sea container trades and spent much of her career on charter to Bell Lines. When photographed sailing from Blyth's south harbour on 11 March, she was working on a weekly service which linked Felixstowe, Rotterdam and Blyth to the Norwegian ports of Larvik and Fredrikstad. Although she has been at work for almost a quarter of a century, she has retained her original name. She has a container capacity of 174 TEU, of which 86 can be accommodated in the hold and 88 (including 20 refrigerated containers) on deck.

(Nigel J Cutts)

There are several features of the ***Northgate*** (GIB, 2071gt/81) which suggest that she was not a product of a European shipyard. In fact she was built in Japan by Kanrei Zosen K. K., of Naruto, and was one of a group of four such tankers built for British owners. The first of the pair, ***Eastgate*** and ***Westgate***, were ordered by Hull Gates Shipping Ltd and delivered in 1979. By the time that the next pair, ***Irishgate*** and ***Northgate***, had been delivered, the Hull Gates company had been taken over by Rowbotham Tankships Ltd. Ownership was later to pass to P & O Tankships and then to the James Fisher group, and it is the latter company's colours which the ***Northgate*** wears as she makes her way along the Manchester Ship Canal on 11 March.

(Dominic McCall)

It is often difficult to keep track of coasters once they the familiar waters of northern Europe but occasionally they are spotted in unlikely places in various states of repair (or, more likely, disrepair). The **Al Riyadh** (498grt/56) is such an example. Built at the Foxhol yard of Th. J. Fikkers as **Jannie**, she was renamed **Capricorn** in 1972, later becoming **Tahmine**. She was purchased by owners in the United Arab Emirates in 1985 and took her current name. When photographed at Sharjah on 19 March, it appeared that her trading days were over.

(Roger Hurcombe)

One wonders where this once-familiar coaster will be spotted in years to come. The **Brendonia** (587gt/66) was one of several coasters built by the Goole Shipbuilding and Repairing Co Ltd in the mid-1960s for J Wharton (Shipping) Ltd, a family-owned company based at Gunness on the River Trent. In 1984, the ship was sold to captain/owner Michael Whiting and her name was amended only slightly to **Brendonian**. She proved to be an excellent ship for Capt Whiting but a combination of poor freight rates in the late 1990s and the vessel's advancing years meant that he reluctantly had to offer her for sale. Some people considered that the ship should be the subject of a preservation attempt but she was sold to Columbian operators although allegedly for service in "Africa". Handed over in Hull, it was a great surprise when her new owners repainted her in full Wharton colours before giving her the name **Shaskia Lee**. As such, she was photographed on 19 March. About ten days later, she left Hull and was reported at Las Palmas in mid-April. Since then, her whereabouts has become a mystery.

(David T Dixon, courtesy ABP Hull)

The reefer **Lyra** (LTU, 2545gt/82) discharges potatoes from Alexandria in Barry's No. 3 Dock, also known as the Dock Basin, on 25 March. This unusual view was taken from Barry Island and is looking eastwards towards Cardiff. Access to the Basin is direct from the Bristol Channel. The refrigerated warehouses on the quayside were built in the mid-1980s for Geest Line whose vessels delivered bananas to Barry from the Windward Islands. Sadly, Geest Line deserted Barry for Southampton in the early 1990s. The Basin is used as an entrance lock for vessels too large to use the normal lock, part of whose chamber can be seen adjacent to the Basin beyond the railings. In the foreground, part of the the eastern wall of the drydock can be discerned; this drydock was last used in 1983. The port of Barry began to see many changes during the late 1990s as the once-extensive docks area was landscaped. Although the volume of trade is much diminished from what it was even a decade ago, there are realistic hopes that the remaining port facilities will witness an upturn in trade at the start of the new millennium.

The **Lyra** was built at Gdynia and retained her original name of **Zonda** until 1994 when she was renamed **Neptunas**. In March 1998, she was renamed **Aqua Fizz** and became **Lyra** later that same year.

(John P Robinson, courtesy ABP Barry/Cardiff)

The chemical tanker **Tina Jakobsen** (DIS, 2401gt/80) is able to carry a wide variety of chemicals in her sixteen tanks. She was built as **Chemtrans Antares** at the Krögerwerft yard in Rendsburg. Lengthened in 1983, she was later renamed **Bird Island** in 1985, **Blue Bird** in 1987, **Multitank Antares** in 1989 and took her present name in 1996. She was photographed as she left Birkenhead and entered the River Mersey on 30 March. *(David Williams)*

The *Fighter* [BLZ, 1560gt/71 is seen laid up in Stanhope Dock, Goole on 1 April. She had arrived in mid-February with a timber cargo from Riga and was subsequently arrested. She lay in Goole until July when she was sold to other Belize-flag operators and sailed as *Laagna*. Built as *Mokhni* she is a member of the 'Spartak' class of about 20 vessels built for the Soviet Union by the Angyalfold Shipyard in Budapest. She dates from 1971 and at some time in her career, her cargo handling gear was removed and her hatches modified, perhaps for use as a container carrier. She was renamed *Fighter* in 1997. *(Richard Potter)*

The wharf on the Dutch River in Goole lies outside the dock system and the stretch of water between the wharf and the confluence of the River Ouse and the Dutch River, although less than a mile long, is difficult to navigate. During the 1990s, the wharf seemed to fall into a state of disuse but as the decade closed it saw a welcome revival of activity. Loading a cargo of animal feed on 7 April is the *Brio* (HND, 678gt/64). This cargo was delivered to Amsterdam and was one of the final cargoes taken by this coaster before she headed for the Danish port of Marstal where she was reported to be laid up by the end of April. *Brio* is her ninth name since she was built by Frederikshavn Værft og Tordok *(Barry Standerline)*

The western breakwater at Swansea provides an excellent vantage point for ships as they leave the port. On 8 April, the **Balmung** (CYP, 2326gt/91) heads out to sea after discharging a cargo of cement. This ship is a product of the Detlef Hegemann Rolandwerft yard at Berne. She was launched and completed under the name **Edith** but appears to have entered service as **Panda II**. She was renamed **Balmung** in April 1999. *(Dominic McCall)*

We have already seen coasters with cumbersome deck cargoes and we now look at yet another one. The **Christopher** (DEU, 2292gt/90) was leaving Dunkirk on 12 April with a deck cargo of four cranes. This coaster has kept her original name since being built at the Detlef Hegemann Rolandwerft yard, Berne. *(John Southwood)*

Even though shorn of her bipod masts and derricks, the **Veprinets** (BLZ, 1968gt/70), ex **Lembit**-98, ex **Basman**-95, ex **Naleczow**-93, is still distinctive as one of the Romanian B452 class built for Polish Ocean Lines. A product of Santierul Naval Turnu-Severin, she was photographed as she passed beneath the Severn Bridge on 15 April. At the time, there was much rust showing on the ship's hull but speckles of red primer paint on the superstructure indicated at least a modicum of care by her owners and crew. Such attention was in vain, however, for the vessel arrived at Aliaga in Turkey for demolition on 28 August. *(Nigel Jones)*

Coaster arrivals at the Orkney port of Stromness are infrequent. The main cargoes are imports of coal and fertiliser, and it is the latter commodity which is being discharged by the **Skantic** on 16 April. We have already seen this coaster on page 8. *(Willie Mackay)*

Both photographs on this page depict coasters involved in the busy cement trades. The **Ronez** (870gt/82) is a purpose-built cement carrier, built at the van Goor shipyard, Monnickendam. She is unusual in being the only seagoing ship registered in Exeter. She was photographed at Magheramorne on 22 April. *(Aubrey Dale)*

There are regular imports of cement to St Sampsons. Guernsey, but the **Askholm** (DIS, 836gt/61) was not a regular caller in this trade. She arrived on 26 April with a part cargo from Seaham, the balance having already been discharged at St Helier, Jersey, and she is seen leaving the next day, bound for the Danish port of Aalborg where the Portland company has a large cement factory. The **Askholm** was built at the Papenburg yard of Jos. L. Meyer as a liquefied gas tanker named **Kirsten Tholstrup**. Sold and renamed **Eastcoast** in 1988, she was converted to a cement carrier in 1996 and took the name **Askholm** in 1997. *(Peter Stewart)*

The *Irlo* (ATG, 1208gt/69), ex *Anta*-94, ex *Simone*-89, ex *Tina*-76, lies at Kristiansand on 2 May. She arrived at the port from Wolgast on 30 May 1999 and was still there in November 2000. She is a member of the Type 58 class from the prolific J. J. Sietas yard on the outskirts of Hamburg. *(Peter Pohl)*

Approaching the port of Boston in Lincolnshire on 2 May is the *Seisbulk* (NIS, 2097gt/84), a ship with an intriguing history. She was one of a class of six or seven vessels built as supply ships for the former East German navy. Surprisingly, there is no agreement about which yard built the ships though it is understood that VEB Neptun Werft in Rostock was the builder. All the ships in the group were sold to a Norwegian owner in mid-1991 and they then passed through the hands of other Norwegian owners, none of whom was able to trade the ships successfully. It appeared that various speculative ventures were planned but these failed to materialise and all the ships have spent periods laid up. The *Seisbulk* received her present name in mid-December 1999, having worked as *Allvang* since 1995. Prior to that, she had been *Marpol Gyda I* between November 1993 and January 1995, and *Eide Rescue IV* from September 1991 until 1993. *Lloyd's Register* and similar Norwegian sources claim that she began life as *Kuhlung* for the East German navy but this is at odds with visual evidence that the *Kuhlung* became *Fjordvang*. There are still some mysteries about this class! *(David T Dixon)*

In recent years, much of the cargo carried between the Channel Islands and the UK mainland has been transferred to trailers which are conveyed by roll-on/roll-off ferries. However, one ship still maintains a conventional service and this is the **Huelin Dispatch** (BHS, 1892gt/78), ex **Stenholm**-96, ex **Visbur**-92, ex **Stenholm**-91, ex **Suderelv**-91. Her construction was unusual because her aft section was built by Norderwerft KG GmbH in Hamburg while her forward section was built by J. J. Sietas, again in Hamburg. She was photographed loading at Portsmouth on 7 May. *(John Southwood)*

The **Fortuna** (NIS, 1094gt/79) was built at the Bijholt shipyard in Foxhol as **Tromp**. Her first change of identity came in 1984 when she was sold to the Arklow Shipping group and she was renamed **Arklow Glen**. She retained this name during her ten year stay under the Irish flag and was then sold to Norwegian owners who renamed her **Fortuna** in 1994. In this attractive view, she is arriving at Perth also on 7 May. *(Richard Jones)*

Built by Santierul Naval Tulcea SA, Tulcea, the **Arion** (ATG, 1846gt/99) still had the appearance of a new ship as she approached the River Usk on 14 May at the end of a voyage from Bilbao. She was heading to Birdport to load a cargo of scrap which she delivered to San Ciprian.
(Danny Lynch)

At the end of a voyage from Rotterdam, the chemical tanker **Clearwater** (NLD, 1631gt/95) passes Tilbury on her way up the River Thames on 19 May. Her hull was built by BV Scheepswerf Lanser at Sliedrecht but fitting out was undertaken by Breko BV Aggregaten & Motoren at Papendrecht.
(Gavin Rayfield)

The number of ships visiting the port of Coleraine is now sadly very much diminished and is limited almost exclusively to exports of scrap to northern Spain. On 25 June, the *Elm* (CYP, 1545gt/79) was photographed as she swung in the River Bann and prepared to head downstream. Yet another coaster built by J. J. Sietas, she began life as *Vera Rambow* and kept this name until 1989 when she was renamed *Waalborg*, becoming *Hydra* in 1993. She was thus named until earlier in 2000 when she was laid up briefly at Oreston Quay in Plymouth. Sold to Anglo Dutch Management Services Ltd, Woking, and renamed *Elm*, she had commenced trading for her new owners only a few weeks before this photograph was taken.   *(Aubrey Dale)*

It will be noticed that some coasters are examples of standard classes built by various shipyards. Such classes not only assist the financial viability of the construction process but they can help owners, too. The *Irene* (CYP, 1010gt/78) is an example of a class of eight ships built at the Barkmeijer shipyard at Stroobos in Holland and she traded under the Dutch flag as *Azolla* until 1993. Proving how well-travelled such ships can be, the December 1998 issue of *Coastal Shipping* shows her at Cape Town but here we see her at Medina Wharf, Cowes, on 25 May having arrived the previous day from Santander.   *(Brian Ralfs)*

A popular location for ship watching is the banks of the New Waterway. The swans, however, are oblivious to the passage of the **Star Anna** (PAN, 1044gt/76) as she heads down the New Waterway at the start of a voyage to Honfleur on 31 May. She was built for Beck's by the Bodewes Gruno shipyard, Foxhol, and was originally named **Viscount**. In 1988, she came under the Red Ensign when named **Canford** and then moved to Irish ownership in 1994, being renamed **Rockford**. In 1996, she was briefly renamed **Lough Mask** before taking her current identity. *(Krispen Atkinson)*

Many ports in Denmark are dominated by large silos used for the storage of agricultural products. Such a silo forms the backdrop to this photograph of the **Deneb** (DIS, 1175gt/81), ex **Kines**-94, ex **Elsebeth Vesta**-86, at Svendborg on 31 May. The letters FAF stand for Fyns Andel Foderstofforretning (Fyn United Feedstuff Company). The ship was built by Nordsøværftet at Ringkøbing. She departed later that day, bound to the River Tees. Svendborg is an attractive port and always has something of interest for those who like small ships. *(Bernard McCall)*

Leaving Chatham for Ipswich on 7 June is the **Sormovskiy 3049** (RUS, 3041gt/83), ex **XI Pyatiletka**-92. She had brought a part cargo of timber from Riga, the balance of the cargo having been previously discharged at Shoreham. She is one of a class built for the USSR in Portugal by Estaleiros Navais de Viana do Castelo. *(Peter Hutchison)*

A dramatic view of the **Greta** (DEU, 1126gt/70) underway in the Kiel Canal on 8 June. Built as **Esso Bergen** by Soviknes Værft A/S, Sovik, she was intended for use as a coastal tanker trading on the Norwegian coast. In 1995, she was renamed **Bjarkøy** and became **Bergen Nordic** and then **Greta** in 1997. Working as a bunkering tanker, she regularly passes along the Kiel Canal in order to deliver fuel to the ferries and ro/ro vessels which serve Russia and the Baltic states from Kiel. She also delivers fuel to ports such as Wismar, Rostock and Lübeck.

(Oliver Sesemann)

The Western Anchorage of Singapore is the location for this view of the **Kabanjahe** (IDN, 1599gt/70). Built by J. Pattje at Waterhuizen as **Irmgard Bos**, she became **Safi** in 1976, then **Tibesti** in 1980, **Aloe** in 1986, and **Angelina** in 1990. It was under this name that she left Piraeus on 1 March 1990, passing through the Suez Canal four days later and arriving in Singapore on 25 March. She was then renamed **Kabanjahe** and seems to have traded between Belawan and Singapore since that time. The photograph was taken on 13th June. *(David Williams)*

Seen in the River Tees on 16 June is the **Rossini** (CYP, 2195gt/98), one of four sister tankers built by Scheepswerf K. Damen BV, Hardinxveld, the others being named **Puccini**, **Verdi** and **Bellini**. They are the largest vessels to have been built at this yard.
(Michael Green)

Hurrying past Walsoorden on her way up the River Scheldt on 18 June is the **Nadine** (ATG, 2862gt/79). Built by Elsflether Werft as **Canopus**, her initial name change came in 1994 when the suffix **I** was simple added to her original name. At the time, she was working on Rotterdam - Ipswich - Hull service. She subsequently traded more widely in northern Europe and had a spell on the Forth Line service linking Grangemouth to Antwerp and Rotterdam. On 9 March this year, arrived at Rotterdam to be handed over to new German owners and since then has traded between Zeebrugge and Antwerp. *(Tony Hogwood)*

The **Connie** (ATG, 658gt/65) lies at a lay-by berth on the Kiel Canal on 20 June. It is now rare for ships to moor at such a berth overnight but it was a common occurrence until a few years ago. The **Connie** was built by Flensburger Schiffsbauges as **Mignon**, a name she kept for five years. In 1970, she was renamed **Franz Held** and then **Jade** in 1982, eventually taking her present name in 1994. Passing the **Connie** is the **Norrland** (DEU, 3999gt/96), launched at the Sietas yard as **Dornbusch**. It is container carriers such as this which have led to the demise of many smaller coasters and which must now be classed as coasters of the future. *(Oliver Sesemann)*

On this page we find two ships which were built at shipyards on Humberside. The chemical tanker **Concorde** (VCT, 2289gt/75) was built at the Richard Dunston yard at Hessle on the outskirts of Hull and worked for ten years as **Pass of Balmaha**. Sold to Italian operators in 1985, she was renamed **Deltauno** and in 1987 she became **Lobelia**. The early 1990s saw her renamed **Lobster**, **Lotus**, **Mare Titanium** and the **Taro** until she took the name **Concorde** in 1995. Although much of her work is in the Mediterranean, she does still venture occasionally to northern Europe and she was photographed at Barry on 24 June.

(Nigel Jones, courtesy ABP Cardiff/Barry)

The **Hope** (BRB, 1785gt/82) approaches Southampton in the morning sun of 26 June. She was one of a pair of sisterships built for John Kelly Ltd, of Belfast, as **Ballygarvey**. In 1990, she joined the Stephenson Clarke fleet and was renamed **Shoreham**, being demise chartered in 1993 to Irish owners although management remained with Stephenson Clarke. She subsequently changed from the Irish flag to that of Barbados and later in 2000 she was sold to Marlin Shipping and renamed **Sea Eagle**. *(Chris Bancroft)*

The **Celtic Endeavour** (BHS, 1597gt/88) was arriving at the home port of her operators Charles M. Willie & Co (Shipping) Ltd when she was photographed on 3 July. She was launched as **Ahmet Madenci II** by her builders, Madenci Gemi Sanayii Ltd, at Eregli in Turkey, but was soon renamed **Iberian Sea**. Owners at the time of the photograph were listed as Iberian Seaways (Shipping) Ltd and she adopted a more traditional Willie name in 1998. Although only twelve years old, she is of classic appearance and evokes memories of a bygone era in coastal shipping. *(Nigel Jones, courtesy ABP Cardiff/Barry)*

The Cornish port of Truro sees far fewer ships than it used to up until the mid-1970s when it was not unusual to see ships berthed at the limit of navigation almost in the centre of the city. The only quay now in use is located a couple of kilometres downstream from the centre but, happily, has witnessed investment during the year under review that ships will continue to sail up the attractive river to reach the quay. There is also every hope of new traffic attracting more vessels. On 5 July, the **Richard C** (DEU, 1298gt/85) arrives to load a cargo of scrap. The ship was built at the Hermann Sürken shipyard in Papenburg on the River Ems. *(John Brownhill)*

A very unusual arrival at Barry on 9 July was the Russian tanker **Kapitan Kovalenko** (RUS, 1881gt/87), built at the Ruse Shipyard "Ivan Dimitrov". Classed as a bunkering tanker, her listed owners are the St Petersburg Municipal Property Committee and it was only in the latter half of 1999 that she appeared in movement reports for international trade. *(Cedric Catt, courtesy ABP Cardiff/Barry)*

Many ship enthusiasts visiting the port of Rotterdam over the years have enjoyed harbour trips on boats operated by the Spido company. In the late 1990s, the departure point for these trips had to be moved upstream to allow the building of a new bridge, the Erasmus Bridge. It was from this bridge that the **Hera** (DEU, 1202gt/75), ex **Herm Kiepe**-96, was photographed as she made her way through the city bound for an upriver destination with a cargo of timber on 14 July. This coaster was built by Werftunion GmbH & Co, Zweigniederlassung Emden. *(Michael Green)*

The small puff of smoke disappearing into the warm summer air suggests that the **Robeta** (NLD, 1372gt/85) has just put her engines astern to move alongside the quay at Sutton Bridge on the River Nene on 16 July. She was delivering a cargo of steel from Rotterdam. It was noted that coasters had ceased to sail up the river and swing off their berth at Sutton Bridge; rather they were swinging at sea to move astern up the river. In mid-December, however, the **Lagik** certainly did attempt to swing in the river - with the much-publicised disastrous consequences. The **Robeta** was built at the Gebr Kötter yard in Haren/Ems for German owners and was originally named **Beta**, her change of ownership and name coming in March 1998. *(Richard Potter)*

The Morskoy class of sea/river ships was built in the late 1960s. Comprising 22 vessels named consecutively from **Morskoy-1** to **Morskoy-22**, it differed from other Russian sea/river ships of the era in that two deck cranes were fitted. The ships have never been frequent visitors to UK and near-continental ports, even after some of them were sold and lost their Morskoy names. The **Morskoy-6** (KHM, 1596gt/67) is unusual for she lost her Morskoy identity in 1979 when she was renamed **Pavel Khokhrakov**. However in early April 2000, she regained her original identity of **Morskoy-6** and transferred to the flag of Cambodia. Construction of the ships was shared between two Finnish yards, the **Morskoy-6** being one of the series built at Reposaari. She is seen at Tilbury on 17 July. *(Ian Wells)*

It would appear that timber imports to Tilbury were particularly prominent in late July for we find the **Ladoga 8** (BLZ, 1511gt/74) approaching the lock entrance on 22 July. Representing yet another class of Russian sea/river ship, she was built at the yard of Reposaaren Konepaja OY, in Reposaari, and was unique within the Ladoga class in that although she was launched as **Ladoga 8**, she entered service under the Finnish flag and named **Norppa**. She reverted to her original name under the Russian flag in 1981, though some sources say 1983. Like several of her sisterships, she has transferred to the Belize flag in recent years.

(Ian Willett, courtesy Port of London, Tilbury)

The **Rauk** (SWE, 1335gt/69) is an example of yet another highly successful standard class built by J J Sietas, namely the Type 58. Introduced in the late 1960s, this class was the first successful large class of container feeder ships. This particular coaster began life on charter to Palgrave Murphy Ltd, of Dublin, and spent the first two years of her life linking Dublin to major continental ports under the suitable name **City of Dublin**. In 1971, she reverted to her originally intended name of **Actuaria** and kept this name until 1976 when she was briefly renamed **Larus** and almost as briefly **Bergvik**, reverting to **Larus** in 1977. She then became **Klinte** in 1984 and finally **Rauk** in 1992. She was photographed just after arrival at Kiel Scheerhafen on 28 July. After visiting the Danish port of Horsens, she returned to Kiel to undergo repairs, eventually sailing on 18 August to Slite.

(Oliver Sesemann)

In Mediterranean coastal areas, the ship enthusiast can never know what lies around the next corner. On 4 August, the photographer was on an excursion coach passing along the Kotor Fjord near Dubrovnik when he came across the **Sipan** (HRV, 375gt/65). Sadly the ship was passed on the "wrong" side but when the road turned back on itself an opportunity for a photograph on the "right" side, and at a higher vantage point, suddenly presented itself. The coaster was built at the Friesland shipyard in Lemmer as **Grada Westers**, her solitary name change coming in 1974 when she was sold to Atlantska Plovidba, of Dubrovnik, then in Yugoslavia. Current registers list her owner as Martin Prkacin, of Dubrovnik, a city which is now in Croatia. *(Jim McFaul)*

Another Mediterranean mystery. The **Zeta** was photographed at the small Greek port of Katakolon on 31 July. This vessel did not appear in any registers or other listings so it was proving difficult to discover her history. The pages of the February 2001 issue of *Coastal Shipping* magazine describe how skilled detective work made it possible to learn that she was in fact built in 1957 at the Travemünde yard of Alfred Hagelstein. Initially named **Dinklage**, she was renamed **Dora Reith** in 1964 and was then lengthened and deepened in 1968 when she took the name **Brise II**. After being renamed **Olaf** in 1983, and **Island** in 1984, she became **Unity III** in 1990. She kept that name for a decade but in 1999 she became something of a mystery. She disappears from movement reports after February 1999 and we speculate that she arrived at Katakolon, was laid up there and was renamed at some stage during the next fifteen months. *(Jim McFaul)*

This view of the **Danica Violet** (DIS, 1088gt/86) clearly shows that her funnel is a dummy - an unusual feature in a coaster. The main engine exhaust pipe, well camouflaged, runs alongside the starboard section of the aft bipod mast. She is a member of a standard class of coasters built at the Danish port of Sakskøbing. Another distinctive feature for a modern class is the fitting of two traditional derricks. The **Danica Violet** was photographed as she left Cardiff on 11 August. *(Nigel Jones)*

The ships owned by Beck's, based at and registered in Groningen, are always maintained in excellent condition. In keeping with coasters generally over the last few decades, the company's ships have grown in size and the **Electron** (NLD, 1923gt/83) typifies the tonnage entering the fleet in the early 1980s. She was built at the Bodewes yard in Hoogezand, and was photographed at the northern French port of Le Tréport on 11 August. *(John Southwood)*

Built by J. J. Sietas, the **Stevns Trader** (DIS, 2433gt/70) traded as **Patricia** for the first fifteen years of her life apart from a brief period in 1976/77 when she was renamed **Scol Action** for the duration of a charter. In 1985, she became **Patricia I** very briefly before her name was abbreviated to **Patric**. In 1988, she became **Baltic Trader** and then **Stevns Trader** in 1993. On 15 August, she was photographed as she passed Tilbury on passage to Antwerp after discharging a cargo of rice at Tilda Rice Jetty, Rainham.

(Kevin Bassett)

Lying on the mud at Giants Wharf, Briton Ferry, on 17 August is the **Inisheer** (IRL, 1839gt/85). She had brought a cargo of rapeseed pellets from Europoort. Built at the Tille shipyard in Kootstertille as **Elisa von Barssel**, she was soon renamed **Flagship I** and this name, too, proved short-lived for she became **Lia Ventura** in 1986. In 1988, she joined the Arklow Shipping fleet and was renamed **Inisheer**, a name she retained until taken on charter in 1985 for a container service linking Rotterdam to Cork, Dublin, Le Havre and Dunkerque. For this service she was renamed **Dunkerque Express**, reverting to **Inisheer** at Rotterdam on 30 May 1999. *(Bill Moore)*

After flourishing in the 1980s, the Port of Pembroke has been operating with a much lower throughput of cargo during the latter part of the 1990s. There are still regular imports of timber from the Baltic, usually brought by Russian vessels. Having discharged a cargo from Riga, the **Sormovskiy 44** (RUS, 2484gt/81) departs from Pembroke for Warrenpoint on 19 August. She is one of a large class of sea/river ships built at the Krasnoye Sormovo yard, Gorkiy. *(Ron Weatherall)*

Until the 1970s, the port of Arbroath on Scotland's east coast was an active commercial port. Since then, trade has declined and it is now used only by fishing vessels although there was one trial visit by a coaster in the mid-1990s. One vessel which is seen regularly, however, is the **Coquet Mouth** (171gt/55), built at the Northwich yard of W J Yarwood & Sons Ltd. Her original role was that of harbour dredger at the coal exporting port of Amble in Northumberland. Since the cessation of commercial activity at Amble, she has undertaken harbour dredging at many ports mainly on the east coast of England and Scotland. *(Barry Standerline)*

The **Solar** (ATG, 2361gt/77) is one of several Japanese-built coasters in this book, built at a time when several owners in north-west Europe looked to Japan for new tonnage. She is a product of the Matsuura yard of Nitchitsu Co Ltd and was built as **Solar**. She was renamed **Marburg** in 1985 but reverted to **Solar** in 1992. The photograph above shows her arriving at Cardiff from Belfast on 26 August, when she was operating a regular service between the two ports. She had been the last ship to sail on the Dragon Line service between Swansea and Belfast which closed on 28 July 2000 and her switch to a different port in South Wales was perhaps no coincidence.

(Nigel Jones)

The **Fosseland** (BHS, 1059gt/79) was built at the Wivenhoe yard of J W Cook & Co Ltd as **Perelle**, her change of name coming in 1994. In late July 2000, she was laid-up for a short time in the River Fal and was sold to Malone Shipping Ltd, being renamed **Malone**. She was photographed as she was leaving the Fal on her first voyage under her new name. It is worth noting that she was heading for Porthoustock Quarry where she became the first vessel to call for over two decades.

(Krispen Atkinson)

A popular place in Hamburg for owners to berth their ships while they await cargoes or undergo minor repairs is the small harbour adjacent to the ferry terminal. Usually the coasters to be seen there are examples of older classes. This was certainly the case on 2 September when the **Steen** (DEU, 328gt/61) and **Iris-Jorg** (DEU, 281gt/56) were photographed. Built at the Hugo Peters yard in Wewelsfleth, the **Steen** traded as **Steenborg** for the first twenty years of her life. Renamed **Ingrid I** briefly in 1981, she became **Steen** in 1982. The **Iris-Jorg** was a product of the Nobiskrug shipyard at Rendsburg and was built as **Eilenburg**. Her next renaming was short-lived for she became **Seestern** in 1964 but by the following year had become **Iris-Jorg**. Both coasters continue to trade actively, generally between ports in Germany and Denmark. *(Dominic McCall)*

The harbour at Cowes on the River Medina which bisects the northern part of the Isle of Wight has two wharves which are visited by commercial vessels. On the eastern side is Kingston Wharf and it is here that oil products are handled in addition to some general cargo. On 5 September, the wharf is occupied by Crescent Shipping's **Blackfriars** (992gt/85) which had made the short voyage across the Solent from Esso's Fawley refinery to deliver a cargo of refined products. Built at the Ringkøbing yard of Nordsøværftet, she was taking a brief break from her normal trading pattern between Milford Haven and Irish ports. She had only recently been painted into the company's new colour scheme, featuring a turquoise hull. *(Brian Ralfs)*

An attractive view of the tanker Polish tanker **Palica** (999gt/77). Built at Stocznia Wisla, Gdansk, she has eight tanks and is able to carry a variety of liquid cargoes. She was photographed in King George Dock, Hull on 9 September. *(Roy Cressey)*

Perhaps because of her distinctive appearance, the **New Generation** (2330gt/66) attracts attention wherever she is. She arrived at Dun Cow Quay, Blyth, on 14 September to lay over for two days before moving upriver to Battleship Wharf where she was photographed four days later. She is berthed with her stern to the quay in order to load a large tractor unit for the hold and a 500-tonne transformer with road rig on deck. The transformer had come from the closed power station at Blyth. Later that day, the **New Generation** moved back to Dun Cow Wharf in order to secure the load before departing for Goole. The ship was built at the Hall, Russell shipyard in Aberdeen as **Kingsnorth Fisher** for charter to the Central Electricity Generating Board for whom she carried heavy cargoes. Renamed in 1990, she is still owned by James Fisher & Sons plc and continues to work for the electricity generating companies which have succeeded the CEGB but is available for other work, too. *(Nigel J Cutts)*

Although photographed far from Europe, the design of the **Juan Diego** (CYP, 1313gt/76) is clearly European. She was built by Frederikshavn Værft as **Charlotte S**, a name which was shortened to **Charlotte** in 1985. Sold and renamed **Juan Diego** in 1989, she has been based in the Gulf of Mexico and Caribbean. We see her at anchor in the Mississippi near New Orleans on 18 September.

(David Williams)

The **Viscaria** (NIS, 1859gt/73) is one of several coasters in this book to have had surgery during her career. Built by J. J. Sietas, she was named **Jurgen Wehr** until 1993 apart from a short period in 1977/78 when her name was abbreviated to **Jurgen W**. In 1993, her name was again abbreviated, this time to **Jurgen** for a short time before purchase by Norwegian operators by whom she was renamed **Viscaria**. Amid these renamings, she was lengthened in 1981 but was more radically altered in 1994 when she was converted from a general cargo coaster to an asphalt tanker, being equipped with four cylindrical tanks for this purpose. She is seen heading for the locks at Holtenau on the Kiel Canal and has been ordered by the control centre to overtake the Norwegian chemical tanker **Bregen**.

(Oliver Sesemann)

The history of the **Skopelos** was unclear until at least partially unravelled in the pages of *Coastal Shipping* in 1999. Built at Hamburg by H. C. Stülcken Sohn, she was delivered to Hamburg-based owners in May 1950. She remained under the German flag but with varied owners until 1975 when she was purchased by Greek interests and renamed **Buena Suerte** under the Panamanian flag. From that point on, her history again is unclear and we do not know when she was renamed **Skopelos**. She supplies the island from which she takes her name, leaving each Tuesday for the Greek mainland port of Volos and returning on Thursdays. The photograph was taken on 27 September. *(Peter Stewart)*

It was in 1998 that the enclosed dock at Port Talbot re-opened for commercial trade after many years out of use. The reason for the revival was the export of granulated slag from the nearby steelworks. Much of this slag had previously been taken away by road transport. Initial cargoes were delivered to the Thames but Glasgow was added to the list of receiving ports and it is the **Loyal Partner** (NIS, 2610gt/79), seen at Port Talbot on 29 September, which has usually taken slag to this destination. Built as **Duro Siete** at the Gijon yard of Sociedad Metalurgica Duro Felguera, the ship has had a surprising number of name changes, becoming **Cabauno** in 1981, **Parayas** in 1985, **Bulko** in 1986, **Parayas** (again) in 1989, **Bulko** (again but briefly!) in 1990 and **Cotalba** in the same year. She managed to retain this name until May 1998 when she was renamed **Loyal Partner**.

(Dennis Shaddick, courtesy ABP Swansea/Port Talbot)

Passing Tilbury Ness on her way down the River Thames on 30 September is the **Fast Ann** (POL, 1740gt/80). Built by J. J. Sietas, she is an example of a Type 104A sea/river coaster and she traded as **Saphir** until 1992. *(Kevin Bassett)*

The Marstal-registered **Juto** (DIS, 969gt/68) was photographed at Scrabster, the most northerly port on the UK mainland, on 5 October. She was built at the Fosnavaag yard of Gerh. Voldnes A/S as **Francia**, being renamed **Tor Francia** when on charter between 1971 and 1973. It was in 1973 that she was renamed **Thunpall I**, a name she retained until 1986. From 1986 until 1998, she was named **Start** and then took her current name.

(Willie Mackay)

Another unit of the Seacon fleet, the **Sea Mersey** (ATG, 1552gt/90) was photographed loading steel at the Orb Jetty on the River Usk at Newport on 8 October. Built as **Remmer** by Mach. Fab. en Scheepswerf Vervako BV, Heusden, her only change of identity came in January 2000. *(John Southwood)*

The weather in the Danish port of Århus was distinctly autumnal on 9 October as the **Barbara** (DIS, 1068gt/66) loaded a wind turbine for delivery to Orkney. This was the first commercial cargo taken by the coaster under this name for she had been renamed from **Lette Lill** only a few days previously. Launched at the J. J. Sietas yard as **Regine**, she was named **City of Antwerp** by her charterers when she entered service and kept that name until 1971 when she reverted to **Regine**. She later became **Carina** in 1975, **Ortrud** in 1984 **Britta** in 1989 and then **Lette Lill** in 1991. *(Bent Mikkelsen)*

A glance at the **Stanelco** (NOR, 1692gt/75), photographed near Larne on 14 October, suggests that she has been converted at some stage in her career and that is indeed the case. She was built by Brattvag Skibsinnredning as the conventional coaster **Siraholm** and was converted to a cable layer in 1982. It was at this time that she took her present name. Her current owners are Alcatel Contracting Norway AS. *(Aubrey Dale)*

The **Eastgate** [GIB, 2072gt/79] discharges a cargo from Grangemouth at the Oil Terminal in Inverness on 20 October. Like the **Northgate** seen on page 13, she is one of the group of coastal tankers built in Japan for the Hull Gates Shipping Company in the late 1970s. She has since been owned by Rowbothams, P & O and latterly Fishers of Barrow but has always carried her original Hull Gates name. *(Richard Potter)*

There were not many shipping movements on the English side of the Bristol Channel on 23 October. The flood tide brought only two vessels, both heading for Sharpness. The first of these, photographed in a rare shaft of sunlight on an otherwise wet and windy day, was the **Konstantin Paustovskiy** (RUS, 2319gt/96) which was bringing 2400 tonnes of bagged ammonium nitrate from her home port of St Petersburg. Built at the Volgograd Shipyard, she represents the latest style of Russian sea/river ships. Her two hatch/two hold arrangement makes her suitable for various bulk cargoes and she has a container capacity of 118 TEUs. *(Dominic McCall)*

The **Kurkse** (EST, 2658gt/97) was photographed as she departed from Wicklow on 26 October after discharging a deck cargo of timber. She boasts a rather complex multinational origin. Her hull was built and launched by Santierul Naval S A at Galatz in Romania but was towed to Oldersum in Germany for completion by Schiffswerft Schlömer GmbH. Registers note her builders as Scheepswerf Damen Hoogezand, Foxhol, in Holland. This typifies the subcontracting arrangements which have become increasingly commonplace during the last two decades of the twentieth century. *(Pat Davis)*

The **Khaled T** (SYR, 2237gt/69) began life as the **Tegelersand**, built at the Heinrich Brand shipyard in Oldenburg. She was sold to Panamanian flag operators and renamed **Astor** in 1981. For the next seven years, she traded between Mediterranean and Red Sea ports and was consequently a regular sight in the Suez Canal. In 1988, she changed hands again, becoming **Polly Prudent** under the Bahamas flag. She was now seen once again in northern Europe for she linked Antwerp, Rotterdam and Felixstowe to Famagusta and Mersin, a trading pattern which continued after she was renamed **UB Prudent** in October 1992. In early summer 1993, she again changed hands, being bought by Syrian owners and renamed **Muhieddine V**, trading mainly in the Mediterranean/Black Sea area once again. Transferred to other Syrian owners in July 1999, she took her present name and maintains similar trading patterns. She was photographed as she left the Syrian port of Tartous on 29 October. *(P W Hobday)*

We stay in the Middle East to look at the refrigerated cargo carrier **Yousef** (PAN, 1973gt/67) at Beirut on 30 October. Built at the De Waal shipyard, Zaltbommel, as **Gorgol**, she was renamed **Isole** for French operators in 1969 and took her present name in 1988. Her present status is unclear for she put into Beirut on 10 November 1997 when on passage from Port Said to Turkey. She was then arrested "on behalf of creditors in respect of overdue payments". She has remained at Beirut for the last three years. *(P W Hobday)*

The **Dalgo** (NIS, 1977gt/71) has had a varied life since her construction at the van Dujvendijk yard in Lekkerkerk. She was built as the **Sassaby** for P & O Short Sea Shipping Ltd, and was a dedicated container ship on this company's services from Tilbury to Zeebrugge, Rotterdam and Hamburg. Sold to Norwegian owners in 1983, she was fitted with a 16-tonne travelling crane and was renamed **Saby**. In 1989, she was sold again, this time to ANS Korntransport II, a company owned by Paal Wilson. Renamed **Dalgo**, she was converted to a self-discharging grain carrier and traded mainly between Denmark and Germany. She was laid up at Haugesund in August 1996 and seems to have recommenced trading by early 1998. By this time she had reverted to the role of conventional coaster. We see her here leaving Arklow Rock Jetty on 4 November. *(Pat Davis)*

As we have noted earlier in this book, one can never be certain which ship is going to turn up after seeming to have "disappeared". Photographed arriving at the port of Aqaba, Jordan, on 6 November is the **Akram V** (SYR, 1461gt/62). She was built as **Tourmaline** at the yard of the Ailsa Shipbuilding Co Ltd in Troon, but there is now no sign of the eight derricks with which she was originally equipped. Changes of name saw her become **Proba** in 1982, **Fergus H** in 1986, **Socotra** in 1987, **Sorocco** in 1990 and finally **Akram V** in 1993. It is at this point that the story becomes more complex. *Lloyd's Register* notes that her class was withdrawn on 1 June 1993 after she had been reported with defects. However, the same ship is noted in *Lloyd's Voyage Record* as trading under the name **Akram 5**. The *Register* has no such listing of her named thus. One cannot be certain of her mechanical condition but she certainly appears to be well kept, at least externally, by her present owners. *(P W Hobday)*

The **Kibu** [MLT, 2187gt/74] is another example of a standard class built for the Soviet Union. She was one of 23 built in Rumania at the Turnu-Severin yard. Launched as **Yunyy Partizan**, she was renamed **Pootsman Kibus** in 1992 after she had joined the Estonian fleet following the break up of the Soviet Union. In 1995 she took her present name. She arrived in Yorkshire at the height of some of the worst floods for many years, but also at the onset of neap tides and her voyage to Goole had to be cut short at Blacktoft Jetty on 3 November. She lay at Blacktoft Jetty until 9 November when tides had improved sufficiently to allow her to complete her voyage. After lightening at the 50 tonne crane berth in Stanhope Dock, she had at last reached her destination at South Dock Terminal on 11 November when the photograph was taken. Too much water everywhere but not enough to float the **Kibu**! *(Richard Potter)*

Now but a shadow of its former self, the dock at Runcorn adjacent to the Manchester Ship Canal nevertheless was host to two coasters on 12 November. One of these was the **Northern Larsnes** (MLT, 2446gt/97), one of a group of coasters built during the mid-1990s at the Slovenske Lodenice AG yard, Komarno, in the country now known as Slovakia. She had brought a cargo of nepheline syenite from Stjernoy in Norway and arrived from Dublin where she had discharged part of her cargo. *(Iain McCall)*

The port of Funchal on the island of Madeira is linked to the Portuguese mainland ports of Lisbon and Leixoes by some six or seven container ships. One of the smaller examples is the **Ilha de Madeira** (PRT, 2749gt/87) built by J. J. Sietas as **Amazone**. She kept this name until her sale to Portuguese owners in 1996. She presently operates a weekly service between Lisbon and Funchal where she was photographed on 20 November. *(Charles Loughlin)*

The unfamiliar background of the port of Alexandria fails to hide the ancestry of the **Sami** (SYR, 399grt/64). She is yet another coaster built at the J. J. Sietas yard, beginning life named **Athene**. In 1976. She became **Freya** and this was altered but little to **Freya S** in 1980. The change was brief for she was renamed **Ellen Fuhr** in 1981, and then **Nadia** in 1983, an identity which she kept for a decade until leaving the German flag and becoming the Syrian **Haidar** in 1993. She took the name **Sami** in 1997. The photograph was taken on 22 November. *(John Filer)*

Dutch shipyards continue to build coasters for owners in Holland who clearly see a future for such vessels despite the vagaries of cargo markets and the seemingly relentless takeover of traffic by road haulage and roll on/roll off ferries. Typical of the 1990s designs from Holland is the **Vissersbank** (NLD, 1682gt/94), built at the Bijlsma shipyard in Wartena. She was photographed at Par on 26 November. She had arrived three days previously from Vlissingen and was loading a cargo for the Mediterranean.   *(Courtesy Port of Par)*

There is no doubt that followers of the shipping scene have to modify their ideas about just what constitutes a "coaster". The number of smaller vessels is diminishing but the number of larger vessels, especially container carriers, dedicated to traditional short-sea services increases all the time. Typical of such larger ships is the **Iduna** (DEU, 3585gt/91), built at the Cassens shipyard in Emden. A container ship with a capacity of 361 TEUs, she has kept this name throughout her life apart from a spell in 1994/95 when she was on charter to the Belgian shipping company Compagnie Maritime Belge by whom she was renamed **CMB Iduna**. She is seen here passing Honfleur on the River Seine on a rather murky 25 November on what was then her regular service between Radicatel and Waterford.

(Dominic McCall)

Observers wishing to trace the **Sea Cross** (BLZ, 2598gt/92) would initially find it difficult to begin. The reason for this is that her name is written as the single word **Seacross** in Registers although it is clearly two on the ship. She was built at the Severnav S A yard in Turnu-Severin as **Alma Ata**, and was renamed **Lieke** in 1995 and **Kometa** in the same year. It was in May 2000 that she took her current name. In this view, we see her in the River Humber on 2 December when outward bound from Goole to Rotterdam. She had arrived at Goole on 26 November after making an 18-day voyage from Odessa. *(David T Dixon)*

Built by Oy Laivateolisuus Ab at Turku, the **Anto** (DIS, 781gt/67) is the only Finnish-built coaster in this book. It is appropriate that her original name was **Finlandia**, a name she retained until she took her present name in 1991. She was photographed as she approached Langton Lock, Liverpool, on 3 December. *(David Williams)*

The last rays of the winter sun catch the **Arold** (VCT, 858gt/65) at Newport on 9 December. Her first name change came in 1976, prior to when she had been named **Horsa** following her construction at the Aukra Bruk shipyard in Aukra, Norway. On this occasion she was renamed **Arold** but when sold within Norway in 1995, she took the name **Trio**. Following fire damage in her accommodation at Stavanger in October1997, she was declared a constructive total loss. However she was purchased and refurbished by other Norwegian owners and reverted to the name **Arold** although now under the St Vincent & Grenadines flag.   (Nigel Jones)

Once again, it was late in the afternoon when the **Union Jupiter** (BRB, 2230gt/90) was photographed as she was loading a cargo of wheat for Belfast. She is one of a class of six similar ships ordered from Cochrane Shipbuilders Ltd at Selby and she was launched on 16 November 1989. In order to meet delivery dates, two of the six were subcontracted to the Hessle yard of Richard Dunston Ltd. The **Union Jupiter** was the lead vessel in the class and was one of three ordered by Union Transport Ltd. Although initial problems with hatch covers were experienced, the design has proved to be successful. Of just under 100 metres in length, they were designated as "Goolemax", being considered the largest ships able to navigate to this inland port. It is worth noting that longer ships have now visited Goole, one of these being seen on the back cover of this book.   (Bernard McCall)

We are nearing the end of our look at coasters throughout the year but surprisingly we have not yet viewed one of the Lapthorn coasters which are frequent visitors to UK and near-continental ports. On 17 December, the **Hoo Larch** (1382gt/92) was photographed as she discharged corn gluten feed pellets at New Holland on the south bank of the Humber. She was constructed at the yard of the Yorkshire Drydock Co Ltd, only a few miles away in Hull on that river's northern shore. *(Carl Dickinson)*

On the same day but on the west coast of England, we find the **Ben Varrey** (IOM, 997gt/86) in Liverpool's Gladstone Lock at the beginning of a voyage to Douglas, Isle of Man, with a cargo of grain. The most modern coaster in the fleet of the Ramsey Steamship Co Ltd, she was purchased from Beck's, of Groningen, in the autumn of 1999. She was built at the Bodewes shipyard in Groningen and had traded as **Triumph** for Beck's. *(David Williams)*

The port of Miami is perhaps best known for the large number of cruise liners which use it. However there is a very active general cargo trade, dominated by container and roll on/roll off traffic, and a variety of other older vessels use the more traditional facilities on the Miami river. An unusual coaster noted loading among the much larger container ships on 29 December was the **Seaboard Spirit** (ATG, 2295gt/85), one of a class of three low air draught ships of distinctive appearance with bridge forward and stern ramp. Built at the yard of Thyssen Nordseewerke GmbH, Emden, she started life as **Anke S**. She spent her early years working on RMS services, notably linking Rhine ports to Boston. She was renamed **RMS Alemannia** in 1992, and then **Dyggve** and **Anke S** in quick succession in 1994. It was in mid-May 1997 that she was renamed **Seaboard Spirit** although she had already been working out of Miami as **Anke S** since earlier in the year. At the time of the photograph she was maintaining a thrice-weekly service between Miami and Nassau.

(John Southwood)

The arrival of the **Vega III** off Guernsey on 28 December caused quite a stir for two reasons. Only a couple of day before her arrival, local newspapers had been reporting the imminent anniversary of the arrival of a much earlier **Vega** at St Peter Port. The latter vessel arrived in 1944 with a cargo of much-needed parcels from the Red Cross to relieve the suffering islanders. The **Vega III**, however, was a real treat for modern ship enthusiasts, although perhaps not fully appreciated at the time. She was the lead ship in a class of six vessels named **Cargo-Liner I** to **Cargo-Liner VI**. This class was to prove to be the forerunner of a host of similar ships, many illustrated in this book, with hydraulic wheelhouses and collapsible masts to permit navigation far inland. The **Cargo-Liner I** was renamed **Bielefeld** in 1981, **Tasman** in 1984, **Noorderling** in 1992, and **Omega III** in 1997. After her owner had faced financial problems, she was laid up at Harlingen in February 2000 and was sold at auction in November to owners who were understood to be Italian.

(Tony Rive)

One glance at the **Carl Phillip** (BLZ, 498gt/43) is enough to suggest that she was built during World War Two and that is indeed so. A product of the Brunswick Marine Construction Co, her original name was **YO 75** and she was later named **Domino** before taking her present name. We do not know when these name changes took place. She was photographed at Port Everglades on 30 December.

(John Southwood)

The low winter sun highlights the ship in this photograph. The **Fast Catrien** (POL, 1740gt/80), a sistership of **Fast Ann** featured on page 42, enters the Alfred Lock at Birkenhead with a cargo of timber from Riga. It seems appropriate that we finish the book with yet another coaster from the J. J. Sietas yard. She traded initially as **Rubin**, her name change coming in 1992. She and other coasters whose names begin with the word "Fast" are comparative strangers to the west coast of the UK, most of their visits being to ports on the east coast.

(Darren B Hillman)

Index of ships' names

Akram V	47	Hoo Larch	53	Ronez	19
Al Riyadh	14	Hope	28	Rosita Maria	13
Alteland	10	Huelin Dispatch	21	Rossini	26
Antares	17	Iberian Ocean	5	Ruza-3	10
Anto	51	Iduna	50	Sami	49
Arion	22	Ilona G	4	Sea Clyde	4,9
Arold	52	Inisheer	35	Sea Mersey	43
Askholm	19	Irene	23	Seaboard Spirit	54
Balmung	17	Iris-Jorg	38	Seacross	51
Barbara	43	Irlo	20	Seisbulk	20
Ben Varrey	53	Juan Diego	40	Shala	3
Blackfriars	38	Juto	42	Shaskia Lee	14
Breaksea	6	Kabanjahe	26	Silva	12
Briarthorn	7	Kapitan Kovalenko	30	Simone	4
Brio	16	Khaled T	46	Sipan	33
Carl Phillip	55	Kibu	48	Skantic	8,18
Celtic Endeavour	16	Konstantin		Skopelos	41
Christopher	17	Paustovskiy	45	Solar	37
Clearwater	27	Kurkse	45	Solway Fisher	7
Concorde	28	Ladoga 8	32	Sormovskiy 44	36
Connie	27	Leonid Leonov	11	Sormovskiy 3049	25
Coquet Mouth	36	Loyal Partner	41	Stanelco	44
Dalgo	47	Lyra	15	Star Anna	24
Danica Violet	34	Malone	37	Steen	38
Duisburg	4	Morskoy-6	31	Stevns Trader	35
Electron	34	Nadine	27	Tina Jakobsen	15
Elm	23	Nandia	3	Union Jupiter	52
Ewald	6	Nariman	9	Vedette	11
Fast Anne	42	New Generation	39	Vega III	54
Fast Catrien	55	Northern Larsnes	48	Veprinets	18
Fighter	16	Northgate	13	Veritas	4
Fortuna	21	Palica	39	Viscaria	40
Freya	5	Pia Theresa	38	Vissersbank	50
Greta	25	Rauk	32	Yousef	46
Gudrun II	2	Richard C	29	Zeta	33
Hera	30	Robeta	31		

Author's notes

As far as possible, the outline history of each ship is given for the benefit of readers who may wish to research the ships featured in more detail and possibly to aid recognition of a ship perhaps seen under a previous name. In common with other shipping books, I have included details of the flag flown by the ship at the time of the photograph, along with gross tonnage figure and year of build. These statistics are the latest available at the time of writing. For various reasons, tonnage figures can vary according to the source used and because the ships themselves are subject to remeasurement. The figures given, therefore, should not be considered as definitive. Flag abbreviations are as below.

Contributions are welcomed for further volumes in this series. Please ensure that your name is written on photographic material, along with outline details of the ship, location and date of the photograph. Any further information which could be used in a caption would be welcome.

Flag abbreviations

ATG	Antigua and Barbuda	KHM	Cambodia
BHS	Bahamas	LTU	Lithuania
BLZ	Belize	MLT	Malta
BRB	Barbados	NIS	Norwegian International Register
CYP	Cyprus	NLD	Netherlands
DEU	Germany	NOR	Norway
DIS	Danish International Register	PAN	Panama
EST	Estonia	PMD	Madeira
GIB	Gibraltar	POL	Poland
HND	Honduras	RUS	Russia
IDN	Indonesia	SWE	Sweden
IOM	Isle of Man	SYR	Syria
IRL	Republic of Ireland	VCT	St Vincent and the Grenadines

Back cover (top) : It is New Year's Day and the **Pride of Veere** *(NLD, 2077gt/99) passes Whitgift on her way down the River Ouse from Goole. She and her sistership* **Pride of Braila** *are the longest ships to visit Goole.* (John S Mattison)

Back cover (bottom) : The last day of the year saw snow lingering on the ground at Sharpness. The **Asseburg** *(ATG, 1939gt/82) was waiting to discharge 2600 tonnes of bagged ammonium nitrate from Kaliningrad.* (Bernard McCall)

ISBN 1-902953-03-7

9 781902 953038

£8.50